THE Queen Mab ORACLE

DIVINE FEMININE WISDOM FROM THE QUEEN OF THE FAE

TESS WHITEHURST

Artwork by MÉLANIE DELON & CECILIA G.F.

THE QUEEN MAB ORACLE
Divine Feminine Wisdom from the Queen of the Fae

Copyright © 2023 Tess Whitehurst

Artworks for Cards 1, 5, 7, 26, and 35 Copyright © Cecilia G.F.
All Other Artworks Copyright © 2023 Mélanie Delon

All rights reserved. Other than for personal use, no part of these cards or this book may be reproduced in any way, in whole or part, without the written consent of the copyright holder or publisher. These cards are intended for spiritual and emotional guidance only. They are not intended to replace medical assistance or treatment.

Published by Blue Angel Publishing®
80 Glen Tower Drive, Glen Waverley,
Victoria, Australia 3150
E-mail: info@blueangelonline.com
Website: www.blueangelonline.com

Edited by Jules Sutherland and Peter Loupelis

Blue Angel is a registered trademark of
Blue Angel Gallery, Pty. Ltd.

ISBN: 978-1-922573-77-3

Contents

Enter the Realm of the Faerie Queen
A Note from the Author   9
How to Prepare Your Deck for Use   12
How to Do a Reading with *The Queen Mab Oracle*   14

The Cards
1. Herein Lives Wisdom   20
2. Protector of the Realm   23
3. Renew Thy Force   25
4. The Sacred Radiance   28
5. Listen to the Moon   31
6. Killed with a Living Death   34
7. Wild, Watery Sea   37
8. The Wrath of Love   39
9. Darkness as a Bride   42
10. Make Not Your Thoughts Your Prisons   45
11. The Rose of Youth   48
12. Strange Invisible Perfume   50
13. A Most Prosperous Perfection   53
14. A Winged Messenger   56
15. Love, Lend Me Wings   59
16. Queen of Queens   61
17. Thee I Will Love   64
18. Proud and Pitiless   67
19. There Is My Pledge   70

20. Thou Art a Witch   73
21. Heart Is Bleeding   76
22. The Spirits Riseth   79
23. Beauteous Freedom   82
24. Spangled Starlight Sheen   85
25. Angelic Fiend   88
26. As Destiny Decrees   91
27. Flower of Warriors   94
28. These Violent Delights   97
29. A Queen in Bondage   100
30. A Vision Full of Majesty   103
31. The Falcon's Flight   106
32. Roses Have Thorns   109
33. Something Rich and Strange   112
34. A Dream of Love   115
35. Everlasting Farewell   118
36. Extremity of Rage   121
37. Welcome, Dread Fury   124
38. The Sea-Maid's Music   127
39. Her Pale Fire   130
40. Love All, Trust a Few   132
41. The Forgeries of Jealousy   135
42. Venus in the Sky   138
43. Raging Fire of Fever   140
44. Follow Darkness Like a Dream   142
45. Dive Into the Fire   145

About the Author   148
About the Artists   150

Enter the Realm of the Faerie Queen

A NOTE FROM THE AUTHOR

The wisdom in each card description comes directly from Queen Mab, the Faerie Queen. Of course, I, Tess, wrote it down. While the card titles are almost exclusively phrases that appear somewhere in Shakespeare's works, the messages contain phrasing and language that I ultimately chose and that sounded right to me. And while they are not without elements of my own beliefs and experiences, fundamentally, I would describe the wisdom as coming through me, not from me. It was a wave of energy that I did my best to feel, understand, and translate onto the page.

Let me give you some history on my relationship with Queen Mab.

When I was a teenager, I became fascinated (obsessed?) with Shakespeare's plays, notably *The Tempest*, *Romeo and Juliet*, and *A Midsummer Night's Dream*.

All three reference magic, alchemy, and the realm of the Fae. While Queen Mab doesn't appear in *The Tempest*, *Romeo and Juliet* features Mercutio's famous Queen Mab Speech; *A Midsummer Night's Dream*'s cast of characters includes the Faerie Queen herself, in this case, referred to as Titania.

In *Romeo & Juliet*, Mercutio spoke jokingly—or

perhaps madly and frenetically, depending on one's interpretation—about Queen Mab. Mercutio's words are fanciful and not particularly complimentary. At best, he portrays Queen Mab as whimsical — at worst, capricious and sinister.

In *A Midsummer Night's Dream*, Oberon, the Faerie King, is at odds with the Faerie Queen. Out of frustration and spite, Oberon plots to enchant her into falling in love with a silly man whose head has been temporarily transformed (also at Oberon's behest) into that of a donkey. Hilarity ensues.

Interestingly, despite Mercutio's uneasy disrespect and Oberon's petty machinations, one still comes away from these plays with a sense that Queen Mab was—and is—a being of immense power and wisdom. At least I did. It was as if Shakespeare and his audience already knew her, at least on some subconscious level, as the Great Goddess: a grand and formidable deity. Perhaps she was a given in their world — a divine feminine manifestation aligned with the earth, the sea, dreams, moonlight, and magic. Like nature itself, she could not be contained or controlled. She could devastate, or she could bless. She inspired fear and awe.

When Queen Mab made it known to me that she would share her wisdom for this deck, I was humbled, delighted, and a little intimidated. I couldn't wait to start, so I could see what she had to say. And I definitely wasn't disappointed. Queen Mab consistently offers deep and valuable insights while counseling us to wield our power without fear or apology. I know I will be drawing upon the magic of this deck for many years to come. It is my hope that you will too.

HOW TO PREPARE YOUR DECK FOR USE

Even if you don't follow the instructions in this section, you can still do a reading with your deck and it will provide helpful answers. But Queen Mab is an ancient being of immense magic. That magic is related to the earth and sky. So if you want to supercharge your readings, perform one of these two rituals. (They are almost identical, except one employs the light of the sunrise and the other the light of the full moon.)

Sunrise Method

On any morning when the sky is clear or mostly clear, gather your deck, a bottle of drinking water or beer, a clean scarf or cloth, and go outside just before the sun rises above the horizon. (Weather apps and sites will provide you with sunrise times in your area.) Find a good sunrise viewing spot and sit on the earth: i.e. any natural surface like grass, dirt, rocks, or sand. If you have a backyard that works for this, great. If you need to find a park or forest somewhere, fine. Just be safe.

Spread the cloth on the earth. Remove the cards from the box and casually shuffle them. This will begin to merge your personal energy with the energy of the cards. As soon as the sun emerges the tiniest sliver, whisper, "Queen Mab, I call on you." Lift the first card from the top and point it eastward in such a way that the image is bathed in the dawn's earliest light. Sense the power of the image awakening as it is blessed by divine light. Then place it face down on the cloth, feeling as you do so that the card is now soaking up the earth's magic. As the sun continues to rise, lift the second card in the same way and then place it face down on the cloth underneath the first card. Repeat with each card.

When this is complete, hold the entire deck in both hands. Touch it to your forehead, heart, and belly. Say, "Queen Mab, as I use these cards, I promise to do my best to hear your wisdom and embody it so that I may own my power and increase the divine feminine magic in the world." As an offering to Queen Mab, pour the water or beer upon the earth. It is done.

Full Moon Method

On a night when the moon is full and visible in the sky, follow the instructions above, only replace the light of the moon with the light of the rising sun. Find a spot where you can see the moon rather than the sun, and angle the image on the card so that it's bathed in the moon's light rather than the light of the sun.

How to Do a Reading with "The Queen Mab Oracle"

It's ideal to do readings in a quiet space where you can be undisturbed, indoors or out. If you'd like to set the mood by safely lighting a candle, burning incense, and/or diffusing essential oil, you certainly may, but this is not required.

Three-Card Reading

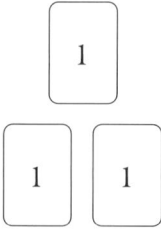

Hold the deck in both hands. Close your eyes. Become aware of your breathing and feel your weight on the earth. Listen to silence and become aware of space. Relax as best you can and inhabit your whole body. Then, bring to mind your question or the situation you are looking for guidance.

You might like to phrase your question as more of a statement about what you'd like help with, addressed to

Queen Mab. For example, "Queen Mab, I need guidance on ____." Or, "Queen Mab, as I decide whether or not to do ____, tell me what you would like me to know." Another option would be, "Queen Mab, what should I do?" Or, "Queen Mab, what am I not seeing?"

You do not need to say please or thank you. In fact, Queen Mab would prefer it if you did not. While politeness is valuable and desirable in most human interactions, it is of no value whatsoever to her.

Shuffle the deck until you feel like stopping. You may experience warmth, tingling, or energy in your hands, or you may just intuitively know when to stop. Don't worry too much about this. Whenever you stop shuffling will be the proper time.

Then, take the first three cards off the top of the deck, laying them out in a triangle: the first card is the top of the triangle, and the second two are the triangle's lower corners. (These second two are interchangeable in importance and can therefore be placed in either position, left or right.)

The first/top card is the main character: the star of the play or the most important thing you need to know. The second and third cards (the cards in the two lower positions) are also important but are supporting roles: they offer clarity and dimension to the primary message provided by the first card.

Take a moment to look at the images before you read each card's accompanying card descriptions in this book. Get a feeling for the figures depicted and the entire aesthetic experience of the cards. What emotions are contained there? What might be going on in the picture? Once you've taken the time to have your own transcendent experience of the images, turn to the page in this book that corresponds with each card and read the wisdom you find there. Notice the thoughts and perspectives that stand out to you the most.

Now that you've read each card's description, consider the bottom cards' relationship to the top card. What similarities are present between the cards? What differences? How might the second and third cards modify, amplify, or clarify the first? How might these subtle interactions and currents of wisdom apply to your situation and question? Don't just analyze and contemplate using your mind. Be willing to allow your whole body—as well as your spirit and subconscious—to absorb the wisdom.

Continue to breathe, gaze at the images, and relax. As you do this, you will bring the wisdom even more deeply into your aura and intuitive, dreaming mind.

Don't feel you need to see all the parts of your answer. The cards may reveal exactly what you need to do, but they also may not. Either way, there will always be mystery. There will always be uncertainty. The point is not to know everything. The point is to allow Queen Mab's deep and ancient current of wisdom to merge with—and eventually become—your own. As you gaze at the images and allow their power to permeate your awareness, trust that your thoughts, expectations, and actions will be shaped by Queen Mab's guidance within the coming days and weeks. In turn, your clear intentions and grounded, personal authority will reshape your world and how it responds to you. In other words, each reading is both a divination and an act of magic.

One more bit of advice: the night after your reading, pay very close attention to your dreams.

One-Card Reading

For a quicker, simpler reading, close your eyes, take some deep breaths and relax while holding the deck in both hands. When you feel grounded and centered, ask your question (see above for phrasing suggestions). Shuffle the deck and remove one card. First, as instructed in the three-card reading section above, take some time to have your own experience of the image. Then, turn to the guidebook section that corresponds with the card and read the words you find there. Notice what messages stand out to you the most as you read.

Weekly or Daily Reading

You can also do a morning reading for general guidance on your day or a weekly reading (perhaps on a Sunday or Monday) for general guidance to keep in mind during the week ahead. For this type of reading, relax, breathe, and then shuffle the deck. Inwardly ask Queen Mab for general guidance on your day or week. Shuffle the deck once more and draw a card. First, gaze at the image. Then, turn to the card's accompanying page in this book and read the guidance you find there. Place the card on your altar or desk, where you can regularly see it throughout the day or week.

The Cards

1. Herein Lives Wisdom

LISTEN. RETREAT. TRUST YOUR INTUITION.

You have access to the wisdom you seek. The Great Goddess has bestowed upon you abundant gifts of knowing, seeing, divining the truth, and hearing the clear inner guidance that will serve you best. She has also graced you with an ability to swiftly cut away illusions, distractions, and tired old conditions you no longer need.

It matters not what dwells in the darkness. You needn't see the pathways that wind through the silhouetted mountaintops or the shaded half of the moon. The Moon Goddess and the power within you will illuminate all you need to know to prevail and thrive. So listen deeply and take action in this moment. The following moments will take care of themselves.

You have the power to *know*. Decisively pull that power back to you now. Or claim it roundly if you have never done so in the past. Your intuitive prowess is a part of you. It is yours. Feel it deep within you. Stand in it, own it, wield it, and radiate it.

In order to recognize your clear inner knowing, it may be helpful or even necessary to pause and retreat from the outside world for a time — perhaps a minute, hour, or day. If you feel an impulse to rush, remember that time is not fixed in the way humans generally perceive it to be. It is responsive and fluid. When you expect it to be in short supply, it will be. But when you expect it to stretch to accommodate you, you will vanquish the illusion that time is your master, and you will instead take your rightful place as the master of time.

So find yourself a quiet and soothing place where you can consciously create some space around the situation at hand. Close your eyes. Take a breath. Take another breath. Relax your body and enter into the silence.

Once you still your mind and relax your body

sufficiently, the answer or direction will be there. You will know what to do, and you will know how to do it with the greatest possible effectiveness and ease.

2. Protector of the Realm

DEFINE YOUR BOUNDARIES. PROTECT YOUR ENERGY.

Being queen is not merely sitting passively on a throne. It also requires actively protecting your realm when necessary. The realm over which you govern is the realm of yourself: your body, your time, your choices, your castle, and your entire domain. These things are a part of you, just as you are a part of them. As such, you are responsible for enforcing the boundaries that keep them safe, peaceful, and thriving.

You know precisely what must be safeguarded at this time. If you think you don't know, take a moment.

Breathe. Relax. Then ask yourself, "If I knew what I needed to protect right now, what would it be?" Trust what you receive. The answer is there for you. So set the boundary or boundaries you need to. Then enforce them valiantly.

This may involve taking action like ending a relationship, leaving a job, or canceling a commitment that isn't aligned with your royal purpose. It may involve speaking your truth to an individual or widely decreeing exactly what you require or will no longer tolerate. In any case, you must also invoke divine protection and guidance. Ask the Goddess to watch over you, your space, a situation, or a loved one and to guide your steps as you continue to steadfastly shield that which you hold dear.

There is no need to be emotional or sentimental about this. You must not believe for one moment that you deserve to feel guilt, shame, or regret for protecting your realm. Furthermore, it is not your duty to imagine or predict what others will think or how they will react. That is none of your concern. What is your concern is standing up for yourself and your realm in precisely the way your intuition is guiding you to do now.

3. Renew Thy Force

REST. RECHARGE. HEAL YOUR ENERGY.

The sun and moon both retreat regularly before once again rising to reign gloriously over the sky. In just the same way, every queen needs downtime to recharge, regroup, revise her strategies, and renew her conscious commitment to her values.

While taking action and moving forward are both commendable behaviors, if you don't stop and let yourself rest, your effectiveness will suffer, and you will do a disservice to yourself and your realm.

On the external plane, the nature of rest is obvious

— it is a mode of not-doing rather than doing. But you are not being counseled to merely sit still or recline for a prescribed number of hours or days. Rather, this card advises you to enter into the emotional and energetic vibration of dynamic renewal.

To say this differently, imagine that you are going into a chamber of colored light (whatever color feels most healing to you at this time), where ethereal and luminescent fae creatures lovingly hover around you like fireflies, shoring up and fine-tuning your energy. In this place, your personal power and auric field are perpetually optimized precisely according to your needs.

This chamber of replenishment is a metaphor for the intentional, vibrational state of vibrant and active renewal. But it's also something you can imagine as a functional inner construct that possesses a spiritual reality. Once you enter it, follow your intuition about how and when to meditate, learn, and gain clarity through writing. Look at your values and clarify your mission. Also, ask yourself what you want in each life area and contemplate actions you can take to help you manifest individual goals. Get honest about the distractions that hold you back, and find ways to limit or eliminate these distractions. Look at the stories you tell yourself about yourself and your desires, and determine how to revise these stories to be even more powerful, joyful, and confident than ever before.

And also, of course, when appropriate, sleep. And dream. Before you sleep, you can set the intention to dream empowering dreams that untangle mysteries, shed light, and bestow profound wisdom and guidance. When you awake, write down your dreams and any impressions they have left upon you.

Take the time you need to sufficiently illuminate, clarify, and empower your inner world. Then, when you feel the inner nudge to rejoin the world of action, you will be a radiant conduit of energy, enthusiasm, and effectiveness.

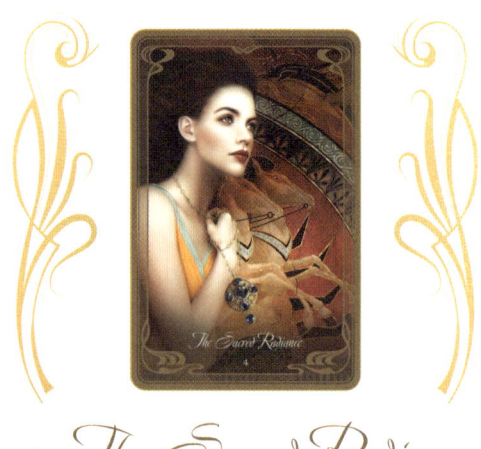

4. The Sacred Radiance

OWN YOUR POWER. CLAIM YOUR ROLE. SHINE YOUR LIGHT.

You are now being called to step into a divinely appointed role. Not a part you will play like an actor on a stage, but a role you will *be*. Even more accurately, a role you *are* — if only you will admit it and locate the courage within you to claim and wield your power.

The sun is not embarrassed about being the light of the world. It does not hide or dim its brilliance in order to be polite. It does not shine with shame. It shines because it must. It is the reigning monarch of the sky because that is what it was born to be. And in its steadfast and undiminished radiance, it blesses the world with life.

Be like the sun and proudly embody the queenlike role that is the truth of who you are.

This may be a message about taking tangible action, steps toward a cherished goal. It may be a passionate wish or desire you have been reluctant to claim or even to admit to yourself as a possibility. Or it may be something you have consciously and deliberately wished for.

Alternatively, this could be a message about internally owning your personal authority, which, in turn, may inspire you to take the lead at work or in your family or community.

Because we are talking about your true divine identity, your own frivolous stories are the only ones that can possibly hold you back. For example, you may be telling yourself lies about your lack of worth or ability, or perhaps you are holding the expectation of rejection, failure, or disappointment. You may be thinking to yourself, "Who am I to do this or that? Why would I imagine that I could even do that? Why would people listen to me, or why would they care what I have to say? What makes *me* so special?" Or, you may be so frozen with terror that you are stolidly refusing to acknowledge or perceive what this is about. Even if you don't want to stay stuck or hidden where you are, it may feel safer than stepping into the light where others might disagree with you, laugh at you, or ignore you.

Whatever the story, it is just a trifle. Unlike your divinely appointed role, it isn't momentous. It isn't eternal. It isn't written in the stars. It isn't even real. So you may rewrite the story or simply decide to release it completely.

You do have a choice in this matter. At the same time, be mindful that—like fire—the power that wants to flow through you can be destructive if not consciously wielded. Ignoring or denying it is not in your best interests. Rather than letting it consume you, take possession of this power and direct it decisively.

Waste time no longer. Claim your identity and bestow upon the world its promised queen.

5. Listen to the Moon

ALLOW UPS AND DOWNS. HONOR YOUR CYCLES.

You will always wax and wane. In the morning, you might feel universal delight, while at night, even fireflies may not give you a thrill. Perhaps on Monday, everybody loves you, but by Friday, no one remembers your name. In May, you could be the uncontested master of your trade, but by November, the world has changed, and you are an apprentice once again.

Progress is not actually predictable. You would be wise to consider yourself lucky that this is so, as a ploddingly upward or forward trajectory would be an abomination — a brutal destruction of wonder, mystery, and delight.

After a summer of romance and magic, the leaves fall from the trees. In time, the bear sleeps, the streams freeze over, and frost dusts the earth like sugar. Some years, a great blanket of snow piles up. In other years, the snow is less forthcoming. Then one day—we can't say which—the bear awakes. Birds sing. Leaves grow, and wind whispers through them. The water melts, and the streams flow. And summer comes again — the same cycle as last year, but by no means the same at all.

Similarly, the moon expands, contracts, disappears, and then expands again. She dances to her own spiraling song. Sometimes the clouds curtain her. Other times she is wreathed in a rainbow. From Earth, we never see her far side. She never reveals all. She keeps her own counsel. She is always an enigma.

And yet, when you get very quiet, you will hear her whisper. You will hear her bid you rest when you are tired and dance when you are wound up. She will urge you to show your face when feeling social and to hide it when you are shy. She will assure you that whether you feel wonderful or terrible—or anywhere in between—the feeling will certainly pass and transform into something else. She will speak to you of ancient magics, and if you need them, she will tell you how to cast the spells that will restore delight, re-awaken dormant wisdom, or revive a frozen heart. She will declare to you that no paths are straight. All paths are crooked and double back on themselves. She will also remind you that true success and authentic riches dwell within your own unique experience and have nothing to do with how other people measure or perceive you.

    Listen to the moon.

6. Killed with a Living Death

Come back to life.

How lovely you look in your pallor and your prison. In a sense, you are dwelling in a shadowy realm in which you are living but not wholly alive. It is striking that even here, you have become queen.

But is this the crown you would choose? As picturesque and regal as your confinement may be, your life is not actually over yet, so wouldn't you prefer your heart beat with passion? Wouldn't you rather be free to wander wherever and whenever you choose? You have certainly sacrificed too much.

It is well known that human emotions can be intolerable. For example, while there has been much lament about the pain of unrequited love, the pain of requited love can also be agony. Loving a mortal being is anguish, for you can never entirely escape the knowledge that every moment with your beloved could be your last. While this can make love all the sweeter, it can also make your heart break too many times to bear.

Similarly, failure can emotionally wreck you, but success will also destroy you if you become preoccupied with the desperate fear that it will end. It's also true that even a life with relatively little trauma will not be free of moments of excruciating sorrow.

Perhaps somewhere along the way—in response to all this pain, memory of past pain, and fear of future pain—you closed yourself down to life, love, warmth, and delight. Perhaps you were unaware that a life half-lived would not, cumulatively, be less painful. For it will be lonelier, colder, duller, and bereft of passionate love.

There is an alternate possibility. You may have faded into this limbo when you began to believe your only viable option was a dead end — a living situation that robs you of your dignity, a job that could never satisfy you, or a partner who doesn't seem to know you or appreciate you for who you are.

Some conditions may take longer than others to

transform or extricate yourself from. Yet, you are not alone. Those chains may seem very real and heavy, but remember the divine authority that comes with your crown. Seek help where you can and do what you must to set yourself free.

Put an end to your mirthless reign as zombie queen. Find the courage to reanimate your living, breathing, laughing self. Reach out for the help of trusted friends, advisors, or healers who will remind you of your worth and power. Call on your divine and otherworldly allies as well.

Rekindle your spirit's fire, and it will bring back the precious depth and sparkle of your gaze.

7. Wild, Watery Sea

WORK WITH THE WATER ELEMENT.

It is as if you are a dehydrated mermaid — barred for too long from the fluid, restorative power of the sea.

I am, of course, speaking poetically as I always do — but I am also speaking literally. As soon as you can, you must go to an ocean, stream, or lake. Alternatively, you might stand under a waterfall or dip your feet in a pool. Even gazing at a public fountain will be healing for you. At the very least, drink plenty of water and prioritize taking a relaxing shower or bath.

This may seem to have nothing to do with what

you are asking. Nonetheless, you must do as I bid. My prescription may seem mysterious, but I assure you it will help to bring about an invisible shift that will open you up to the direction, certainty, and outcome you seek.

In addition to the above guidance, this may also be a message about starting a career related to water or moving somewhere closer to a river, lake, or sea.

We cry tears of saltwater when we are overcome. The more we let our feelings flow, the more our old pain transforms like jagged rocks breaking down into soft and yielding sand. When you breathe fully, consciously, and repeatedly into your heart and belly, it will help you feel and heal emotions previously hidden or stuck.

The underwater realm is a place of creativity, poetry, music, and dreams. In the sea, you can go not just east and west, north and south, but also up, down, and every which way. What's more, water doesn't move in straight lines; it spirals and swirls. Swim along with the tide — engage in creative pursuits, sleep deeply and long, and record your dreams. Or simply retreat into your own revitalizing depths for some quiet alone time and loving self-care.

Be a landlocked mermaid no longer — presently, find your way to the wild, watery sea.

8. The Wrath of Love

OPEN YOUR HEART. DROP YOUR DEFENSES.

Love has hurt you. Now you are on a mission to hurt love back.

Tragically, both humans and faeries can fall prey to the impulse to lash out at those we most care for, or even to preemptively punish those we would perceive as potentially withholding the love, support, admiration, or approval we desire.

In romance, we become jealous, or perhaps our partner says something in a tone we hear as truculent, sarcastic, or dismissive. We might even be responding to a relationship that has long passed, and our old pattern is resurfacing in another guise. Instead of allowing our tenderness to be seen and felt—which might help us heal the confusion at the root—we escalate the situation to all-out war by insulting, rejecting, or avoiding the very one we care for.

It is especially unfortunate when you actively desire love. Yet because you have been so hurt or disappointed by love in the past, you see all would-be suitors through a veil of suspicion — and therefore reject them, attack them, or even avoid meeting them altogether.

The same pattern can be at work in friendships, social situations, and any personal, career-related, or creative pursuit in which you would like your essence to be noticed and admired (and we would all like our essence to be noticed and admired). Such preemptive defensiveness happens when you cannot open your heart wide enough to let yourself be seen because you fear that if you do, it will only be wounded or excluded once again, which (you believe) would be too much pain for you to bear. Yet you do not realize that you have become the one who is doing the rejecting. You may think others are being cold to you, yet it could be more accurate to say that you are being cold to them. Perhaps they are responding to your chilliness in kind, or maybe you are projecting an imagined tone or attitude onto them and mistaking your impression for absolute reality.

If you choose to, you can spend an entire lifetime in the wrath of love. But if you truthfully want the companionship and camaraderie you profess to, you must leave your poison arrows behind.

9. Darkness as a Bride

BE ADAPTABLE. DESCEND INTO THE DEPTHS.

I was there, and I know — the goddess Persephone was not abducted by Hades. She went willingly to marry her love. Being crowned Queen of the Underworld was her cherished destiny.

It is true that for half the year, she stays in the Summerland, bathing in sunlight, walking barefoot in green meadows, and wearing flowers in her hair. But it is also true that during this time—the Spring Equinox until the Fall Equinox—she secretly pines for her shadowy realm. She is most in her element when she reigns over her dark domain. The lush and velvet darkness is her home.

You can learn much from Persephone's fluid adaptability and the fearless delight she takes in the dark.

Persephone is well-versed in eternity, so she does not shrink away from the obvious truths humans so meticulously attempt to deny. She can sit with a dying man with unflinching compassion. She can hold a crying mother who is grieving for her only child. When a spirit leaves the body, she can pick that spirit up and valiantly carry them through the veil.

For mortals, your kind can be bizarrely squeamish about mortality. When the sun is shining brightly in the sky, you can almost make yourself believe that death is a tragedy that will not befall you — other people, perhaps, but not you. Not your children. Not your partner. Not your friends.

And so you do not live fully. Without the experience of winter, how can you appreciate the spring? And then, without soaking in the sensory beauty of the summer, how can you pass into the fall with serene satisfaction? Why would you willingly relinquish a luminous awareness of the endless cycle of life and its stages — birth, life, death, and rebirth? For this awareness is wisdom.

Whether you allow for the inevitability of death

or forbid it from your mind, death will not spare you. It will not spare anyone. So why fall out of step with eternity and lock yourself out of the kingdom of your joy?

Similarly, unmask grief, and you will see it is none other than love — the most excruciating edge of love. You can deny your grief only to the extent that you can deny your love, which is to say — you cannot. Not truly.

When you brush against something you fear to experience or gaze upon, do not shut yourself off from your power. Find your courage. Descend into the deep, receive your crown, and be transformed.

You must never cling to the light exclusively. Like Persephone, every faerie queen is a creature of darkness too.

10. Make Not Your Thoughts Your Prisons

FREE YOURSELF FROM LIMITING STORIES.

Your mind is detaining you in a cage of its own making. You are tied up in intricate, beautiful chains of thought. But just as you have unknowingly imprisoned yourself in these illusions, now you can knowingly set yourself free.

If it's not apparent what thoughts are posing as handcuffs, chains, or prison bars, ask yourself, "What trap do I seem to be in? How is my cage showing up in my inner or outer world? Do I seem to be in a situation I don't like? Is there a particular worry or thought pattern I can't seem to get out of my mind?"

Perhaps you feel as if you have to do something you don't want to or be someone you don't want to be. Examine your beliefs, and identify the ways you are unnecessarily limiting your freedom.

Sometimes, you believe you can read other people's thoughts, and then you feel constrained or drained by what you imagine they are thinking about you or wanting from you. You see someone looking at you sideways, and you feel certain they are judging you and finding you lacking when it is just as likely that they're quietly admiring your hair. Or you mentally go over and over something you said, believing that you've accidentally offended someone by how you phrased something when it's highly possible they were never the least bit offended at all.

As intuitive as you may be, you are not impartial enough to accurately guess what others are thinking about you. So you may as well get out of the habit of trying. Not to mention, a queen must be who she is and behave as she behaves. Not everyone will approve, and some will indeed be offended. But to reign effectively over your realm, you must learn to put aside your worried imaginings about what others are thinking. It's not your job to be a mind reader. Trust others to speak up on their own behalf. And if you feel compelled to know what they are actually thinking, use your voice and ask.

Social expectations and norms, too, can work their way into your mind and proceed to behave like a jail. Your human culture is a maelstrom of brightly deceptive magic — wicked poetry and visions that steal your power by making you believe you are too large, too small, too old, too young, too beautiful, too plain, or some other such despicable lie.

You can be kind and respectful to others without minimizing who you are or denying what you want, and you can be fully present in your culture without falling hopelessly under its spell. There is no scenario, however, in which you will please or placate everyone. If you attempt to do so, you will succeed only in driving yourself mad.

Make not your thoughts your prisons. Make your thoughts your wings, and ascend.

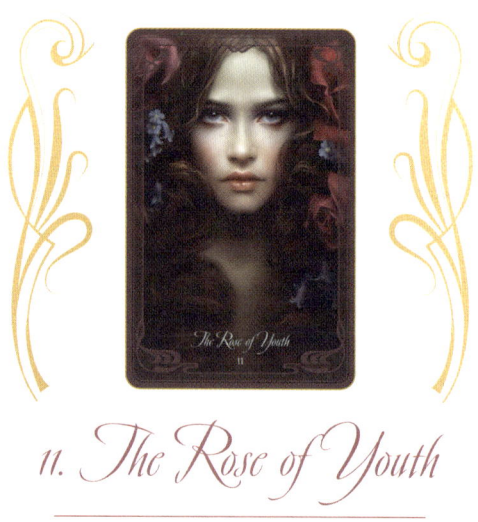

11. The Rose of Youth

LET PASSION SHOW YOU THE WAY.

Youth is like a fragrant rose blooming and a bright fire burning. Youth's very fullness contains a threat. A fire threatens to violently consume everything in its path. A flowering rose threatens its own assured and deliberate end.

It is said you cannot call back to yourself the dangerous pleasures and passions of youth. The petals fall. The fire burns itself out. The winds of time blow the remnants away.

And yet! And yet — there is always the chance

that another rosebud will bloom. There is always an ember in the soul that may still ignite into a flame. Youth itself may be fleeting, but caches of its magic remain.

Regardless of your present age, there is youthful passion here — a spark that may ignite into a fire, a bud that may yet fulfill the breadth of its lush and fragrant design. Perhaps you're asking about a romantic relationship, a creative project, a life direction, or something else entirely. Whatever it is, there is a corresponding ardent desire within you that seems to have a life of its own. That ardent desire will show you the way.

A caveat: as you follow where your passion leads, consciously braid patience and wisdom into your action. For a youthful passion is by its nature unstable. In youth, you have no experience of the vast unfolding of time, so you are loath to delay your deeds through learning, negotiating, and problem-solving. Look at poor Romeo, who hastily swallowed poison mere seconds before he might have learned that his Juliet, in fact, still lived. In so doing, he robbed them both of precisely that which was most precious to the other.

My advice for you, then, is twofold: let your fiery fervor bloom, but do not let your impulsiveness rush you forward into ruin. Temper the wild ardor of youth with the prudent standpoint of age.

12. Strange Invisible Perfume

WHO DO YOU WANT TO BE?

Your unique personal essence far transcends the visible. It is as if, wherever you go, you wear an ethereal cloak of unseen color, fragrance, and light.

It is an ancient mystical practice to learn how to magnify and adjust the effect of your presence, which considerably impacts how others perceive you and respond to you. In the fae realm, we call such magic 'casting a glamour'. To some extent, you already cast a glamour when you select the colors and fabrics you wear, apply cosmetics, and adorn yourself with jewels. But you can intensify the benefits of such efforts by drawing upon your magical authority and intentionally choosing the qualities you wish to emanate.

Is this a form of deception? I do not think so. It is more accurate to say it is an art: a playful way of expressing who you are. And you are a jewel with many facets. Some days, you will feel like letting one facet shine, and other days, another. But all the facets are yours — in fact, there are countless facets of you that you haven't yet recognized, claimed, or explored. Sometimes, you must experiment with a facet before you recognize it as your own or as an intermediary step to uncovering a quality or combination of qualities that are even more authentic to your soul.

For example, when a new queen is crowned, she does not feel like a queen exactly - not at first. She must wear the crown for a good while before her royal identity begins to feel like her own. But in the meantime, she actually is queen, and so she must be queen. It is in choosing to wield her power now that she finds her way to wield it more and more masterfully throughout the duration of her rule.

What role are you stepping into, or what conditions would you like to attract? When you enter a room, how would you like that room to light up around you? What do you want people to see? How do you want them to respond? What positive changes do you want to make in the world by using your influence, and why are these changes important to you? What new facet are you now uncovering and allowing to shine?

Once you know the answers to these questions, you can build your glamour within and around you. You can do this with your cosmetic and sartorial choices (conscious adornment is powerful magic in its own right). You can also do this by finding the qualities you desire within or pulling them toward yourself in your spiritual work.

You might light a candle. Look into a mirror. See yourself as you want the world to see you. Say words to yourself that confirm and solidify that image. If there's someone you admire who has held a similar role in the past, you can ask yourself what she would do — how she would walk, how she would speak, the subtle ways she would inspire others to listen, and the authoritative choices she would make.

Imagine a bright, energetic essence—a strange invisible perfume—emanating from you and powerfully affecting how you are perceived.

13. A Most Prosperous Perfection

EXPECT ABUNDANCE.
APPRECIATE BEAUTY AND BLESSINGS.

Monetary wealth and general abundance are on the horizon for you now. To usher in these blessings with the greatest possible ease, conjure a sense of expansive gratitude and present-moment opulence.

When you delight in the bounty and beauty surrounding you, you will naturally attract even more of the same. The simplicity of this axiom makes it no less true — you become wealthier when you appreciate the wealth you already have.

Your physical body alone is a luxurious gift. When you pay attention to your senses and make a point of enjoying textures, colors, tastes, sounds, scents, environments, music, and just the electric aliveness of being in a body, you are, of course, instantly rewarded with pleasure. But you also open up magical channels to receiving more and more such pleasurable rewards.

It is true that in your human culture, the topics of wealth and luxury are burdened with complex layers of painful narratives: stories of scarcity, class, greed, entitlement, hunger, guilt, envy, and disenfranchisement. In many cases, these stories are not just stories — they are also real experiences of poverty, inequality, antiquated religious programming, and crushing injustice. You may have had such experiences yourself, or your ancestors may have passed on some of their lingering horrors to you.

You can honor the truth of these past experiences without unwittingly allowing them to hold you back from receiving the abundant flow of resources that is your due. First, allow yourself to become conscious of the challenging emotions and beliefs you harbor about wealth and success. For example, notice if you feel resentment toward people with more money than you have, if you believe it is intrinsic to your identity to struggle financially, or if you believe that wealth requires a backbreaking amount of work. Look for any and all stories that may be paving the way for disempowerment, and write them down. Then question them, dismantle them, and compose new, different stories about wealth that empower you rather than keep you saddled with lack.

Also, look for the wealth you already have: the clean water that runs through your pipes, the roof over your head, the food in your kitchen, and the clothes you especially love to wear. Even if your current bank balance is relatively small, see if you can feel grateful for the money you do have. Also, look for or cultivate a feeling of bounty when you laugh, spend time with loved ones, and engage in activities you enjoy.

Finally, be careful not to measure your wealth against the wealth of others using external indicators of status. The definition of wealth is not the degree to which you can impress others with fancy, stylish, and expensive things. Wealth is simply knowing that by your own intrinsic standards of comfort, stability, and enjoyment, you have enough.

14. A Winged Messenger

PAY ATTENTION.

This particular situation, endeavor, relationship, or time of your life carries a vast, eternal, inter-dimensional importance.

For further insight into how this message applies, look deeply at the luminous being here portrayed. Imagine for a moment that she indeed lives. She is near to you, although not visible with your physical eyes. She does not employ human language, and yet she has something significant to communicate. Close your eyes, relax your body, and feel her presence. Once you believe you can sense her—or once your imagination has even slightly conjured her up—open your eyes and read on.

This ethereal spirit arrives in response to a life experience that reverberates throughout lifetimes, planes, and dimensions, in multiple directions of time.

If you listen to her silence and feel her closeness, you will receive a clue as to what this means for you. Below, you will find some possibilities to help illuminate her message, which is actually a reminder of something you already know.

- You may be healing an issue that has been with you through multiple lifetimes.
- You may be encountering an ancestral issue or another ancient pattern of energy that has pulled you into its sway.
- Your current circumstance could relate to your sacred lineage: a spiritual vow, practice, or talent you have carried forth into this lifetime from the distant past.
- You may be engaging with someone you previously knew by another name and face at a time when you also had a different name and face.
- It's possible that you are fulfilling your destiny or now have the opportunity to change your

fate into a destiny.
- It's also possible that you are in a portal of transformation: the actions you take (or don't take) now will reverberate for many beings, for many eons, in many dimensions.
- What feels familiar to you here? What feels like something you've been waiting for or expecting? What feels like something you've always known?

Did any of the above examples stand out to you? Did the words visibly light up, or did their particular sounds resonate in your mind?

If you aren't sure of the winged messenger's significance yet, don't worry. That's why she's here. Close your eyes again. Breathe and relax. Listen. Feel. Hear. Go beyond linear analysis and intellectualizing and allow yourself to sense a deeper and more resonant spiritual truth.

15. Love, Lend Me Wings

LET LOVE CARRY YOU.

Love, indeed, has lent you wings. Those wings can carry you swiftly to new worlds and dizzying heights.

So why do you feel uneasy? Because in your heart of hearts, you know that flying too high can be dangerous, your wings are delicate, and the desired outcome of your daring errands cannot be guaranteed.

And yet, of course (of course!), you must fly.

What is this love that has lent you such wings? Who or what do you love so passionately that it both electrifies and haunts you? It could be a child, a sweetheart, a discipline or craft, or a glorious vision of your future you know you must find a way to actualize.

Whatever it is, you have cause to celebrate. Experiencing love like this is what will allow you to one day look back on your life and know that you have lived.

So embrace this love. Let it carry you upward and onward, perhaps to your desired destination, or perhaps to another one that has not been foretold or foreseen.

Take action on the dream. Tell your sweetheart how you feel. Break your heart wide open with love for your child every day.

If you're unsure what step to take, or you don't believe you could even begin to move toward your desire, no problem. You must shift your reality in a way that opens portals of possibility. The heart is the great alchemizer. Breathe into your heart, follow its guidance, and allow your world to transform.

The only thing you must not do is stay where you are out of fear. There will be fear. For humans, where there is love, there is always fear. But here is the secret: your love must transcend it.

Spread your wings, open your heart, and fly.

16. Queen of Queens

BE THE BOSS.

Tap into your true, inherent authority and wield it now.

True authority is not what you say, how you say it, what you wear, or how you carry yourself. Your authority may inform such choices, and sometimes such choices can help you locate and tap into the authority within. But true authority is not equivalent to the choices themselves. It is not on the surface. Rather, it is transcendent, vast, and deep.

Here's something else about true authority: it is

never desperate. If you find yourself feeling desperate to be liked, desperate to be approved of, or desperate to be seen or heard in any particular way, you are not owning or standing in your power. So you must take a step back, recalibrate your motives, and let that desperation die.

Sometimes you tell yourself that you are not desperate when actually, you are so desperate that you can't even bear to admit your desperation to yourself. For example, have you ever met someone you perceived to be powerful and immediately disliked or resented them before you even gave them a chance? Why did you feel that way? Because you wanted their approval so desperately, you hated them for it. Or perhaps you were envious of their esteemed responsibilities or role. Either way, you were selling yourself short. You were not embodying your intrinsic nature as queen.

A queen living in her power does not meet others with rudeness or disdain but with expansiveness and grace. She does not feel the need to put on a show, so she does not flail around in an attempt to impress or entertain. Even when someone treats her disrespectfully, her trust in her royal status is such that she does not feel diminished. Perhaps she will set a boundary, remove herself from the situation, or speak a necessary truth. She will do so with an inner quiet and confident calm that easily broadcasts her authority, more quickly and thoroughly than indelicate blustering or amateurish snobbery ever could.

Here is a secret you must always remember. While it is true that you are inferior to no one, you are also superior to no one. True graciousness is found in a belief in universal equality — you rule your realm, just as others get to rule theirs. If you are constantly measuring your status alongside the status of others, it is because you do not actually believe in your power, so you must continuously look for flimsy and subjective evidence of it in the outside world. This is exhausting for you. It is also based on the lie that human culture is a 'rat race.' You are not a rat. It is beneath your dignity to believe such a lie.

My words may sound severe, but the news is good: your authority is divine and eternal. Begin by knowing this. Your most confident steps and auspicious choices will surely follow.

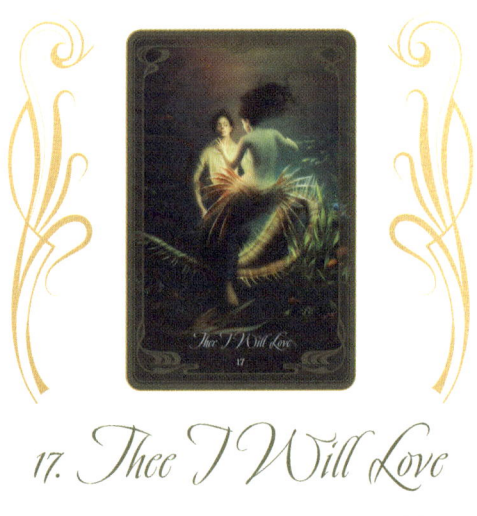

17. Thee I Will Love

COMMIT TO TRUE PARTNERSHIP.

You do not live in the shallows. You are a creature of the wild and mysterious deep. And you have pulled (or are about to pull) someone beautiful into your exotic and magical world.

A part of you might wish for a universally accommodating partner. One who never fails to dote on you, agree with you, and give you everything for which you ask. But you would quickly grow tired of such an arrangement. You do not desire a servant or a devotee. You desire an equal.

There is tension between equals — particularly those who are attracted to each other or who desire to build or create something beautiful together. This is not to say that you should ever tolerate or justify mistreatment or abuse. It is just to say that when you pull someone you care about into your world, you must expect to be drawn into their world as well. Sometimes this will involve disagreements and conflict as you learn how to navigate the waters of your relationship together. But most of the time—if it is a relationship worth keeping—joy and harmony will reign. This will include laughter, passion, inspiration, and mutual support.

And often, the discord you experience will eventually spark healing, fresh perspectives, and empowering new ways of being that you never previously could have imagined.

This relationship may indeed be destined to last a lifetime. But even if it is not, it is a significant step on your journey. It is an opportunity to love. So do not hesitate to show someone your world — to share what you are passionate about, describe your past experiences and how they have shaped you, and open your heart to trust. In turn, be curious about your partner's world as well. And commit to the wild and unpredictable journey of letting your worlds collide.

It is wonderful to find someone with whom you

connect. So follow the impulse to summon them down into your watery lair. Be bold, decisive, and unapologetic about who you are, but do not seek to manipulate or dominate. Allow the other person their freedom. And be willing to swim up to your partner's realm above the waves, even if that occasionally requires you to leave your comfort zone behind.

Be curious. Be brave. Go deep. And see where this partnership leads.

18. Proud and Pitiless

SPEAK YOUR TRUTH. STAND UP FOR YOURSELF.

Now is not a time for compassion or compromise. Do not seek to demonstrate how easygoing, permissive, or accommodating you are.

On the other hand, there is probably no need to be rude. Rudeness is often a response to feeling resentful, which in turn is a response to believing that someone else holds power over you. And you must never believe such a thing. To do so would be to willingly and unnecessarily place yourself in a position of weakness.

Instead, behave like a queen and simply stand

up for yourself. Clearly state what you require in this situation, including what you know you deserve and what you absolutely will not tolerate. Then, be ready to enforce those conditions and boundaries, even if doing so means you must make a bold move, such as taking legal action, resigning, or walking away.

Do not be drawn into manipulative games that seek to destabilize your clear sense of self. Be vigilant. Do not allow a certain tone of voice, a subtle facial expression, or sneakily chosen words to cause you to question whether you are justified in making reasonable requests and demands.

Be aware that past conditioning can undermine your personal authority. For example, if you were raised to believe you should always smile and be 'nice', you will worry that asserting your power will upset people or cause them to dislike you. The truth is, it may upset people. It may cause them to dislike you. But you must learn to override your fear of these things by valuing yourself more than you value the thoughts and opinions of others. Now is a precious opportunity to practice.

Set the clear intention to be true to yourself in this situation and in all situations that follow. Every time you exercise your power in this way, you will feel emboldened. Your energy field will light up with your inherent spiritual force. You will learn to seek out situations that nourish you and reject situations that deplete you. Over time, you will find it easier and easier to take unapologetic action on your own behalf, and your star will continually ascend.

19. There Is My Pledge

Transform pain into action.

There is significant pain in your past. You may even feel that your pain has shaped and defined you — your personality, preferences, and life experiences.

Perhaps you feel intense anger or sadness in response to past misfortune or mistreatment. Or, you may have emotionally closed down and instead feel numb, lethargic, or even depressed. It's possible your unprocessed or unhealed feelings around past trauma have crystallized into a particular resentment that feels inherent to who you are. This may manifest as an obsessive vendetta against a belief system, social paradigm, or political group that you perceive as embodying all that is wrong with the world.

The god Chiron was dubbed 'the wounded healer' when he learned that his personal pain could serve as a portal to express compassion for others, which in turn helped them to heal. And while this could never ease his pain, it nevertheless brought him a significant measure of peace. In the same way, you are now presented with an opportunity to channel pain from your past into present-moment positive change.

When you do this, old, stuck energy within you will start to move. Imagine tossing a match onto a dusty old pile of firewood. Suddenly what was once dull and dead becomes cleansed and alive with blinding flame and light.

If you're unsure what such a transmutation would look like for you, tap into the places in your mind, body, and spirit that feel frozen, bitter, enraged, fearful, or crippled by pain. Breathe into those areas. Don't shrink away from them or tense up around them. Cry if you need to, become incensed, or allow whatever feelings arise. When you feel ready, ask yourself, "What am I passionate about? Who needs my help? Whom can I offer to heal? Whom do I want to protect?"

Your answer to these questions will illuminate

your next step. Close your eyes. How do you see yourself expressing your newfound passion to heal, serve, or protect?

You might feel inspired to join or organize a social or political movement. Or, perhaps you already do something—such as art, therapy, medicine, police work, parenting, or teaching—that will be reinvigorated when you underscore your action with your guiding purpose. It's also possible that you'll feel compelled to embark on a new activity or endeavor or to enroll in a university or training program that will assist you in bringing your most treasured vision into form.

You may have been a victim in the past. You may have felt limited or disempowered by your past hurts or misfortunes — but never again. Your courage is even now transforming you into a formidable force. Henceforward, you are a warrior.

20. Thou Art a Witch

WORK YOUR MAGIC.

You need fear no one and nothing. You have the power to transform this situation into one that pleases you.

When the witch goddess Circe discovered her magic, she began to fashion her world according to her will. While she was only one goddess among many distinguished divinities, she was cunning and resourceful. She always found a way to work with what she knew and what she had to protect and emerge victorious — even when she tangled with the wiliest humans and the most powerful goddesses and gods.

For centuries, witches were feared and loathed more than we were respected or esteemed. So you may believe that if you were to unapologetically exert your power and influence, you would be seen as unattractive, unlikable, or even evil. You might fear that people will whisper behind your back or shun you or that you will end up alone and lonely.

Maybe, this paradigm has become so entrenched that you have willfully denied or unknowingly suppressed your power out of fear. Well, no more.

You are the authority in your world. So, what would you like to experience? In what ways would you like to feel freer? In what relationships would you like to shift the balance of power?

Circe transformed a rival nymph into a sea monster and a crew of trespassing sailors into a drove of pigs. When she was banished to an island, she made it into her idyllic domain. Your transformations may not be as dramatic. But if someone currently appears to be a rival, a trespasser, or a tyrant, or to otherwise stand between you and your desired reality, transform their role. A rival, trespasser, or tyrant can become any number of things: a friend, ally, peer, subordinate, or simply someone from your past whom you never need to worry about or interact with ever again.

Once you determine how you would like to transform a relationship or another aspect of your world, relax. Breathe consciously. Clear your mind and come into the present moment. And when you feel ready, listen to the clear inner guidance that bubbles up from the deep.

You may feel guided to seek out and perform a spell or ritual to change how you perceive or approach this situation, to ask for a specific variety of help or support, or to embody your power while clearly visualizing your ideal success. Or, you might feel compelled to do all of these things.

You have an abundance of transformational wisdom and power available to you. Access it now.

21. Heart Is Bleeding

BE KIND AND COMPASSIONATE TOWARDS YOURSELF.

You have become so invested in an imposing commitment, standard, belief, fear, or self-image that you have forgotten to notice or value how your heart feels.

First and foremost, tend to your heart. Acknowledge where you are suffering. Be mindful of the ways you feel exhausted, inauthentic, out of your element, or out of alignment with your values. Perhaps you are spending significant time in an environment that doesn't nourish you or around people who don't actually know you or want you to thrive. Or you may be hiding your true personality or preferences — not just from others but also from yourself. It may also be the case that you need to take some downtime to rest, journal, and become aware of your true feelings and desires.

Once you take time to listen to yourself, you may discover that you will benefit from making a major change — such as leaving a relationship, study program, or career or perhaps embarking on a brand new path. Or, you might want to stay where you are, but to do so authentically, you need to make some changes in how you show up or interact.

You could be operating under the assumption that a relationship or life choice will only work if you completely or partially conceal who you are. That assumption is self-defeating. Here's why: If you choose to stay in the situation without making any changes to how you approach it, you will undoubtedly begin to feel drained. On the other hand, you may abruptly leave the situation before you actually know whether or not it's a good match for you.

The only solution is to be transparent and genuine. Have a potentially uncomfortable conversation — state what you need. Open up and let your true feelings and desires show. Set whatever boundaries feel right to you. And see what happens. Some situations and relationships will be in harmony with you. Others won't. But you can't know unless you give yourself the opportunity to find out.

Have compassion for yourself. Remember your value. Take the time you need to reconnect with your heart. Allow your feelings to be what they are without judging them. And then follow your heart's clear direction.

22. The Spirits Riseth

FEAR NOTHING.

Do you know why magicians summon demons and the dead? I will tell you a secret — it is not for the reasons they often profess. It is because there is great power in becoming the master of one's fears.

Children worry about the monsters hiding under their beds. When the lights are extinguished, are ghosts hiding in the dark?

In truth, each and every one of us holds authority over the invisible realm. We each get to say what we will allow in our environment and what we will not. We each get to command the spirit realm to act in accordance with our will.

The opposite paradigm—the belief that we must constantly tremble in fear of evil spirits and unruly demons—has been born and perpetuated through stories told by leaders who would seek to keep their people weak, dependent, and afraid.

Possibly, somewhere in your vast and shadowy psyche, you are still a slave to such fears. Otherwise, fear of another variety is gnawing away at you and feeding on your power. Will people like you? Are you good enough? Is the world a lonely place? Is the universe random and indifferent? What if you run out of money? What if you become ill or get in an accident? Is society beyond repair?

Become acquainted with—and honest about—the sneaky fears hiding under your bed and lurking in the dark. From now on, they are your servants. You must be their master.

You are no longer a child. You have the necessary wisdom and authority to reject a fear-based belief system. What's more, you are resourceful. You are wise. You can't know what the future holds, but you can know that whatever it is, you can face it with equanimity, clarity, and aplomb. Relax your body, breathe deeply, and find the baseline of single-minded certainty within you.

Now, call up your old fears. Don't run from them — invite them in. And find the power there. Greet them with courage, and they will transform. Speak to them with authority. See how they simper and cower before you.

Raise the spirits. Conjure the ghosts. Invoke the demons. Henceforth, they are your minions. They will never again rule you. Command them and revel in your power.

23. Beauteous Freedom

ADMIT YOUR FEELINGS.
BE YOURSELF. FIND YOUR PATH.

Beauteous freedom is on the horizon for you. But in some significant way, you are not quite free. Not yet.

You have been running from something: a deep pain that you don't want to feel or haven't had the time or space to safely feel in the past. Or, you have been so focused on succeeding or surviving that you have been ignoring the wild spirit that is absolutely vital to who you are.

In some cases, you may be experiencing an

addiction. That addiction may have been born out of a desire for freedom, but now it only serves to keep you captive to its demands.

In other cases, you may have locked down your creativity, desires, and sense of adventure. You may be limiting your food intake in a harsh manner, judging or denying your sexuality and sexual desires, or refusing to allow yourself any relaxation, playfulness, wildness, or fun. Maybe you have an idea about what it means to 'be a good person', and that idea does not include your natural irreverence, wanderlust, curiosity, or rebellious spirit.

But you need live this way no longer. Now's the time to get honest about how you are perpetuating your own personal imprisonment. Then, make the changes that will free you. Step out of your self-imposed confinement. Question your ideas about what it means to be 'bad' or 'good'. Where did they come from? Are they realistic? And how are they keeping you enslaved?

Everyone is mean sometimes. Everyone is greedy, jealous, awkward, and petty. Everyone sometimes feels worried and alone. Everyone occasionally wants something they can't have. And everyone often wants things they *can* have that won't hurt anyone for them to enjoy. Release all shame about sharing in these universal human experiences. Stop trying to rise above them, ignore them, or use them as reasons to emotionally isolate yourself, elevate yourself, or deny yourself love.

Your beauteous freedom is a fundamental part of you and is accessible to you now. Tap into the energy of freedom and allow it to guide you in finding your way back to yourself.

24. Spangled Starlight Sheen

SEEK AND FOLLOW DELIGHT.

There is a special magic here, or one is soon to be revealed — a mysterious radiance, a beckoning beauty, and an otherworldly shine.

There are times and events in one's life that take on a special luminosity. Destined paths cross. Ancient memories are awakened. A fog of monotony lifts, and everything glows.

It could be that you have recently met someone with whom you have a soul connection. Alas, this card does not reveal the destiny of your relationship with this person. It cannot, for mystery is a vital ingredient here. You must not unveil the mystery but rather surrender to it. Let it take you where it will.

It is also possible that you are newly fascinated by a passion of some kind: an artistic discipline, an intuitive art, or a magical spiritual path. Something with spirals upon spirals and depths upon depths. Something you could study or practice for lifetimes and never possibly learn or discover all there is to know.

Or, the idea of moving to a particular region or making another major life change may be inexplicably— yet undeniably—dazzling and enticing to you.

Whatever the case, you will know what to do when you follow the ancient and hypnotic melody of delight. Open up your senses and your heart, and make yourself available to this moment and all the beauty it contains.

Beauty can be shallow and fleeting. But there is another type of beauty that is infinite — divine, eternal, and accurate. It is a beauty that calls you toward itself. You can ignore such beauty, or you can shun, minimize, and devalue it — but why would you choose to live in such a way?

Let go of needing to see the end of this path, for there is no end. Give up on making reasonable choices, for reason does not rule here. Do not expect others to cheer for you as you dance, for the song that guides you is one that only you can properly hear.

    The fascination you feel is a gift. Treasure it.

    Where shall you go? Simple. Along the path of your sparkling, shimmering bliss.

25. Angelic Fiend

CLAIM YOUR DESIRE. SATIATE YOUR TRUE CRAVING.

An intense emotion or desire won't leave you alone. It may be a fixation on another person, an insatiable hunger for attention, an obsessive need to achieve a certain kind of success or even a craving for an unhealthy substance or behavior. Whatever the longing, what if you stopped trying to suppress, hide, ignore, or imprison it and instead let it speak? When you do so, you will uncover vital information that will, in turn, allow you to call back the fullness of your power.

If you're not quite sure what desire this card refers

to, perhaps you feel that life has lost its luster lately or that your sense of purpose or enthusiasm has fled. That's because you've hidden this desire from your own self, and doing so has snuffed out the fire of your joy. Simply asking yourself what passionate impulse is burning within you will easily bring it to your awareness. So go ahead and do that now. Close your eyes and ask, "What overpowering desire have I been hiding from myself? What do I feel is lacking?" There may be tears when you admit what it is your heart is pining for so fervently. Let them flow.

    When you're ready to let the great and terrible longing within you speak, have your journal nearby as you light a candle. Gaze at the flame. Sense its heat and feel the resonant sympathy of the burning flame of yearning within you. Breathe deeply. Feel the fire expand in your belly and heart. Let it rage. Keep breathing through any feelings that may arise. Then, with curiosity and reverence, ask this inner inferno, "What is it you really want?" Then write. Don't wait until you know what you will write. Just start writing. You might start with the words "I really want..." and see what comes.

    Keep writing until you go beyond the surface appearance of the desire and tap into the core essence of the need. Look for the feeling you want to experience rather than the outward manifestation of the yearning or how you think it will look when you get it. For example, if it appears that you want a certain person to want you back, keep writing until you discover that the true essence of the need is simply to love and be loved. If it appears that you crave a certain unhealthy behavior or substance, keep writing until you discover the basic need to feel supported, healed, nourished, or safe. (Of course, these are just generalizations for the sake of illustration. You must find your own truth in your own time and way.)

This is not an exercise in shaming yourself for the shape in which your desire has appeared — quite the contrary. It's an exercise in inviting this desire—exactly as it is—to your innermost sanctuary and then listening with clear-eyed, compassionate attention until you hear and understand the cry for love at its heart.

The fiend within you is actually an angel. It is guiding you toward what will most nurture you now. Listen to it and give it what it wants, and you will finally feel satiated, powerful, and at peace.

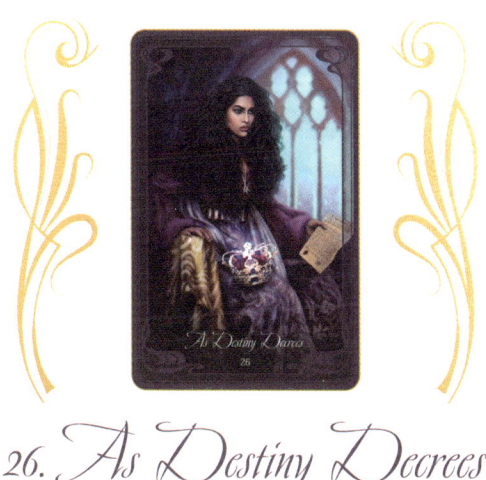

26. As Destiny Decrees

EMBRACE THE UNEXPECTED.

Destiny is taking you in a direction you did not foresee.

It is as if, all your life, you have been struggling and striving to be queen — or perhaps you were groomed for such a role. But as soon as the crown was placed upon your head, you received news that it was never yours in the first place. That path and that title were not intended for you.

A relationship is not what you thought it was. An opportunity evaporated or transformed into something else. A pathway took an unexpected turn.

Is this development shocking to you? Is it really? Or deep down, did you know there was something else in store? Something else life was navigating you toward? Somewhere else your heart of hearts wanted to go?

Truthfully, you would not have thrived spending your life indoors, sitting on an uncomfortable throne, with a window perpetually separating you from the moonlight. You are wilder than that — freer and far less tamed. You are a creature of nature: the elements and the cycles of the earth. Surely you knew this. To wield your magic to the extent it deserves, you must chart your course and make your own way under the open sky.

It can be disappointing to be forced to relinquish a tidily planned destiny. There is safety and comfort in walking a road many others have walked before. It is natural to mourn what will never be. Still, rest assured that the adventure ahead of you is lovely. If you step into the unknown with courage, you will never look back with regret at the path that wasn't yours to take.

The Great Goddess and your many helpers in the unseen realm are here for you. Call on them. Request their support to move forward into your divinely designed destiny. You may not know what that destiny holds for you yet, but that makes it all the more exciting.

Let go of your ill-fitting crown — it may have

looked pretty, but it always weighed heavily on you and caused your head to ache. Surrender your hold on what you once thought may have been. Leave old rules and expectations behind. Find your freedom. Draw upon your magic. And then step out into the fresh air and glorious night.

27. Flower of Warriors

EMBODY YOUR POWER.

Some flowers manage to defy the odds and flourish under harsh conditions, such as high elevation, extreme winds, and the driest desert soil. Some grow through the cracks in concrete. Others bloom when there's still snow on the ground.

You are such a flower. You may have been through wars, droughts, famines, blizzards, and floods. You may have been pummeled by circumstances beyond your control. You almost certainly have been hurt. In so many ways, you have been forced to find your own way and learn as you go. But rather than perishing, you have emerged strong, beautiful, and filled with light.

Draw upon your hard-won strength. It is there for you. And don't just draw upon it; revel in it. Take joy in it. Wear it like a gorgeous gown. Let yourself radiate your well-earned authority like a queen among queens. Goddess knows: you've earned the right.

Perhaps you did not realize how splendid you have become. Maybe you believed all those trials and tribulations would permanently damage you and bar you from living a life of empowerment and joy. Such beliefs would be false. Look now within and see how the immense pressure has not crushed you — not in the least. Rather, it has transformed you into the rarest of diamonds. A diamond, remember, is famous for its beauty but also for its strength.

Never be ashamed of what you have been through. It has made you who you are today: a flower that may appear delicate but is not that at all. A diamond that both shines like a star and cuts like a knife.

Your past challenges give you the ability to be warm, empathetic, and compassionate. And—when necessary—they also allow you to be cold, tough, and unyielding. Luckily, you are intuitive about what point in this spectrum it is appropriate to embody at any given moment. Whenever you act on this clear and subtle inner knowing, victory and glory will be yours.

It is high time for you to wear your strength proudly, like a crown. When you do this, you will be unstoppable. You will be brave enough to open your heart to divine love. You will be courageous enough to speak your truth confidently and take aligned action without apology. You will be fierce enough to follow your dreams with unbending focus, hunt them down, and make them yours.

Oh, and if you're wondering whether you should step into a new role as a leader of some kind? The answer is yes. You should. You will be legendary.

28. These Violent Delights

SEE THROUGH THE DRAMA AND GAMES.

You have been drawn into a drama — something seductive, exciting, and dark. Perhaps you haven't realized there is a form of beauty in this because you have only been focused on the drama's requisite heartbreak or discord. But the beauty is there.

Sometimes we actually crave drama in order to inject a little excitement into life. This is not a judgment. In fact, life would be half-lived if it didn't contain at least a little such delectable enchantment and pain.

But the message here is that conditions are

unstable. As they are, they certainly cannot hold. Someone may be drawing someone else into a lovely trap. Are you the trapper or the trapped? Most likely, a little of both. But take heed — if things continue as they are, a glorious shipwreck could be ahead.

One day, you might reminisce, smile, and say, "It happened, it was terrible, it was also lovely (in its way), and then it was over." Or, perhaps you would prefer to prolong or preserve something here by establishing more sustainable conditions. If the latter is the case, you have work to do to transform this situation or relationship into one that will happily and joyfully last. Even still, you may not succeed. In fact, it may be better for you to look elsewhere for stability — to take what you will from this experience and move on to the next.

Provided engaging in this drama is not truly dangerous to your body, mind, or spirit, feel free to stay with it for as long as it thrills and entices you. It will probably not last much longer anyway, so you might as well live it up. But if engaging in this drama does put you in some form of danger, or if you've just grown weary of being in such an unsustainably elevated milieu, get out.

Another reason to put a stop to this situation would be if you are mistreating someone or cruelly playing with their emotions. If you are not acting with integrity, other areas of your life will surely suffer. You will do well to change your approach so that you act with greater honor and impeccability, even if that requires you to apologize or admit you have been dishonest or behaved untowardly.

As the great bard wrote, "These violent delights have violent ends." If you aren't ready for an ending, you must find a steadier pace and navigate toward calmer waters.

29. A Queen in Bondage

LIBERATE YOURSELF FROM CO-DEPENDENCY OR NARCISSISTIC CONTROL.

A person, group, or situation may be siphoning off your power.

At first, this may have seemed like a desirable arrangement for you. Perhaps you were flattered by the attention, enraptured by the possibilities, or otherwise believed the relationship, collaboration, or agreement to be respectful, productive, or mutually beneficial.

Alas, things were not what they seemed. Looking back, perhaps you can see there were warning signs.

Whether you can or can't, you must forgive yourself. No one escapes this life without—at one time or another—being disappointed or disillusioned. Berating yourself won't help. Neither will punishing yourself by remaining in chains indefinitely.

Your best course of action involves two steps. First, admit you are in a bind; then consider your friends, family members, and allies. Also, consider others who might be able to assist you in getting out of this situation — physically, mentally, or emotionally. Who do you know, or who might you enlist, to help unlock your chains and set yourself free? Ask that person (or group of people) for help.

Do not omit the asking. No queen has ever defended her crown without the help of counselors, protectors, healers, and champions. And even queens take missteps or make choices they later regret. We all must be able to reveal our vulnerabilities to at least a trusted few, so we can receive the support and guidance we need.

Someone may try to convince you that you have an obligation to stay in this situation one more day or until some future event occurs or old debt is repaid. Do not believe this.

You are a winged being by right—light, bright, joyful, and free—like a seagull in sunlight, designed to soar above the sparkling waves. Call your true nature back to you now. Invoke the support you need so you can step out of your bondage and fly.

30. A Vision Full of Majesty

Answer the call. Take devotional action.

Trust your vision. Give credence to your clear inner knowing. Take a stand for who you are.

Time and again, cultures, religions, kingdoms, and families have attempted to teach their youth that they were wrong — wrong in their dreams, desires, or goals; wrong in their intuitive knowing or spiritual orientation; wrong in their sexual or gender identity; or wrong in their love. Sadly, some carry this false, disempowering dogma, in some form or another, into adulthood and beyond.

Perhaps you are now examining something fundamental to who you are (or aren't). Or, perhaps you are struggling with or looking closely at a work situation or relationship dynamic. For example, you may feel irresistibly drawn to take a particular path but believe that taking this path would go against what is expected of you or prevent you from receiving external validation or support from someone important to you. Perhaps it would even put an end to a relationship or remove you from a cherished role.

Your guidance here is clear — you must fulfill your vision for yourself and your life. Tune in to that vision now. What does it feel like? What does it look like? Where might it lead? You will likely not be able to see the entire picture, but once you have a sense of your vision's form and texture, you must seek to fulfill whatever your vision asks of you. Let nothing stop you from doing what you do and being who you are.

There will always be some who fear change. And there will always be some who herald and make way for change — those whose bravery helps usher it in. If everyone always went along with the crowd and did what they were told, imagine how backward and un-evolved we would be and how many injustices we would still suffer. This is a time when you must make your own way, despite the odds and despite any apparent opposition. Doing so will ultimately bring great benefits — to you, others, and the world.

In your heart of hearts, you already knew all this. All you have received here is validation. But that is enough.

31. The Falcon's Flight

CULTIVATE OR CLAIM YOUR MASTERY.

Artful mastery is vital to your present-moment experience.

There are two possibilities here. The first is that you have spent much focus and many long hours mastering a skill of some kind (spiritual, practical, artistic, emotional, or career-related) that it will benefit you to draw upon now. The second is that it will bring you great joy, satisfaction, and success to commit wholeheartedly to a particular discipline or practice — to start where you are and begin working toward greater and greater competency and skill.

Reflect for a moment and decide which of these two possibilities is most accurate for you now.

If you have already achieved a significant degree of mastery in some important area, you will thrive if you put this mastery to good use. Have you fully recognized and acknowledged how hard you've worked and how far you've come? If not, do so now. All your hard work has not been for nothing. While you will likely continue to learn and hone your abilities throughout your lifetime, the fact remains that you've succeeded in what you set out to do, which was to become an expert at your chosen craft. So choose now to own and claim your prowess. Wield that prowess with confidence, and you will bring about the conditions you desire.

On the other hand, if you believe it is time for you to channel your hard work and determination toward future mastery, what form will that mastery take? Relaxing, playing, experimenting, and enjoying the journey of life are all lovely and important pursuits. But now it is time for you to choose a clear direction and go all in. Once you know what you are committing to, create structure. Decide when you will practice, how often, and what you will do when you practice. Find teachers or mentors you trust. Adopt habits that support your ultimate aim. Look for role models and study those who have walked this path before. How would you like your unique form of mastery to look, specifically? Of course, it's natural for you to adjust your course as you go, but to get started, it will be helpful to make a plan that includes your ultimate goal, intermediate goals, a timeline, and also the major practical action steps you will take.

Becoming an expert at something, by its very definition, is not easy. It takes time, focus, and diligent effort. But hard-won excellence—proficiency that goes beyond the pale—feels like nothing else on earth. While at times it can admittedly feel like a slog, at other times it can give you a sense of transcendence — as if you are flying, as if you are divine, as if nothing in the world can ever stop you.

You are ready. Step on the path to mastery or be the master you already are.

32. Roses Have Thorns

TRANSCEND PRICKLY DEFENSES AND COURAGEOUSLY CONNECT.

A rose's thorns are not proof of her sharpness but of her voluptuous sweetness that is too rare, too full, and too generous to go unguarded.

Similarly, many precious souls were gravely wounded in their past, causing them to erect daunting defenses against people or situations that may otherwise wound them yet again.

You are one such soul or you are presently encountering the barbed barricade of such a one. Or perhaps both these statements are true.

For those with emotional scars or wounds, love is often hidden behind formidable iron: bars, locks, safes, and swords ... or—to use yet another metaphor—a maze. Like a labyrinth of cold metal, a relationship can take time to navigate from its austere outer rim to its welcoming innermost heart. If you are determined and lucky enough to finally reach the center, it will likely look very different than the place where you began — warm and soft rather than cold and hard.

To come full circle with our metaphors, you will have endured the thorns long enough to discover the rose.

While a prickly dynamic may be showing up for you in a romantic relationship, it can also show up in friendships and work relationships and even with regard to your personal goals and desires. Your hackles may rise any time you are afraid of getting hurt, abused, disappointed, slighted, embarrassed, or abandoned. Of course, this is just as true for others as it is for you. You will be wise to ask yourself, "Who has their defenses up in this situation and why?" Is it you? Is it someone else? Is it both?

Don't stop looking when you discover the thorns. Look further, for the rose is there as well.

Have compassion with yourself and others for

the past pain that has lent itself to these forbidding defenses, but do not continue to give your power away to the illusion that such defenses are all there is. Place your attention not on the prickly thorns but on the velvety softness of the rose, even if you can't quite see it yet. Breathe into your heart and be brave enough to let its radiant vulnerability shine. Your heart's light will open up the heart of the other — the person, group, or situation. Then you will see truly, be seen fully, and deeply connect.

    Know this: love is more important than safety. Vulnerability is more precious than power. True courage is never the protective prick of the thorn — it is always the fearless generosity of the rose.

33. Something Rich and Strange

ACCESS THE INFINITE. DISSOLVE INTO ONENESS.

Even when your present human body perishes and dissolves into dust, your eternal soul will survive. The radiant light that carries you through dimensions and lifetimes is indestructible. It is beyond the very fabric of time and space. It was never born, and it will never die.

The same is true for all sentient beings. All are one with The One.

Identify now with your true, eternal self rather than your illusory, transient, temporary self. Draw upon the power of your soul's infinite light. Transcend limitation and find peace by remembering who you really are.

If a loved one is no longer in the physical form you knew them, or if a loved one is about to transition out of this realm and into the next, connect with that loved one's eternal self. Know in your heart that you will not be separated, because you never were and never could be. You are as inextricably connected as rays of sunlight or waves on the sea.

The convincing appearance of your mortality means you are destined to suffer and grieve. This is what it means to be incarnated into form. No matter how hard you try, you will feel the pain of your seeming separation. But the more you identify with your infinite nature—your soul's pure light that is one with divine light—the more freedom, wisdom, comfort, and power you will find.

Learn to live on both levels — the finite and the eternal. It is like watching a play: the world of the play has its own relative reality—its plot, its setting, and its characters—in which you choose to invest for your own temporary enjoyment. But simultaneously, your reality is larger, more real, and more inclusive than the play. You care about what happens in the drama, but you know it is only for a limited number of acts, and once these acts are complete, the lights will come up, and the world of the play will fade.

    Employ the same dynamic in your fleeting mortal life. Be invested in the character you are playing and the friends, lovers, and foes that surround you in your earthly revels. But don't be so invested that you don't know, all the while, that these revels most certainly will end. The thin air (the pure light, the infinite being) into which the actors melt is the divine mind, with which you—and I, and everyone, and everything—are one. There will come a day, in the finite realm, when we will leave not a rack behind. But we will not truly be gone. We will be what we always were — infinite.

34. A Dream of Love

BE MINDFUL OF BOTH TRUTH AND ILLUSION.

There is no love so complete, so idyllic, as a love for someone largely unknown.

When your time with someone dear to you has been limited or brief, you can readily perceive within them every fair and noble quality. If you love a stranger, or someone you know only minimally, it can appear that this person is made of pure magic. They bring joy and delight to your soul. You feel intoxicated when you so much as picture their face. You may consequently become infatuated or obsessed.

There are two sides to this. One is truth, the other illusion.

In truth, we are all infinite, angelic, god- and goddess-like creatures. We are beautiful. We are brave. We are thoughtful. We are clever. We are shards of a divine and radiant mirror, possessed of every shade and sparkle of the spectrum of the sacred.

The illusion is what obscures the other truth — that we are none of us perfect. Most of us are very far from it. While all the light *is* within us, it does not all have the privilege of shining. Some of the lanterns are broken. Some of the stars are obstructed by clouds. Some of the candles have been extinguished by rain, and others have been blown out in the wind.

And yet, when you see the perfection in another—or when someone else sees it in you—miracles often happen. More light shines. More lanterns are lit. More stars are visible. More candles are illuminated. Seeing the truth of one's perfection helps that truth to spark, radiate, and ignite.

On the other hand, with time, relationships progress. If a relationship moves past the idealization stage, it changes into something else: something less delirium-inducing, but more sustainable — less sugary but more sweet.

You might say that when one's imperfections

become visible, the romantic whirlwind slows. In the most desirable scenarios, it becomes a gentle, nourishing breeze.

But sometimes, relationships do not substantially progress past the idealization stage. When the mask of perfection falls away, one or both partners may not like what they find beneath it. Or at times, there is no real partnership, so there is never an opportunity to remove the mask at all.

Still other times, or at other points along the path, a relationship may still have much to offer, but one or both partners becomes temporarily disenchanted and looks elsewhere for that luscious bliss that follows in a new love's wake. There can be great danger here of trading in a great and venerable love for a flashy—and fleeting—new one.

Here there is truth, and there is also illusion. If you are wise enough to perceive both at once, you will hold all the wisdom you need.

35. Everlasting Farewell

SAY GOODBYE.

Why is autumn so radiant and its light so golden? It is the season at the summer's end. It is a glowing goodbye to yet another happy spell of sunlight, growth, life, and warmth. Its fleeting nature reminds us of the passing beauty of this life and the ephemeral nature of all the pleasures it contains.

Something is now passing out of your life permanently: a friendship, a past endeavor or dream, or a cherished chapter of your life. Faced with the ending of something, you can often see how divine and lovely it always was. Both past and present take on a luminous quality. If you are noticing that quality now, let it open your heart. Bravely feel the sweetness and the sadness of moving away from something special you have experienced and loved.

It can be difficult to say goodbye forever. But that is what you are doing now, or what you must do.

If you are ending a romantic relationship or friendship that isn't right for you, you must truly end it. This is not a time to desperately cling to an ideal you know in your heart is no longer possible, or never was. We cannot tell our emotions what to do, so love or rage at this person as you must. But be willing to let them go. And then follow through.

If someone is ending a relationship with *you*, respect their wishes to do so. Let go. Grieve. Feel the fullness of the pain that is there. But be willing to bid a grand and final adieu. You do not need this person or this relationship. You will be fine without them. In time, in fact, you will certainly prosper and thrive.

If a loved one is passing out of the material realm of the humans and into the ethereal realm of the spirits, you are indeed saying goodbye to the human form forever. But you are not saying goodbye to their eternal essence. That—like love—can never dissolve or die. Grief will be present, of course. Always, always, breathe into the pain. Let it blossom like a rose within you. Trying to avoid pain or shrink away from it is not brave, but cowardly. And it will only cause you to suffer more. But all the while, remember that you will never be bereft of this person's essence. Their body was finite, but the love and laughter you have shared is indestructible. It is beyond time and space. It abides without end.

So wave and blow kisses to the temporary form that is now passing away. Let the pain be as a bracing fall wind — chilly but invigorating, a breeze that inevitably blows into every life. And treasure the love that remains.

36. Extremity of Rage

FEEL YOUR ANGER.

Rage is only shameful if you think it so. In its way, it can rush through you like beauty or pleasure, much like the sparkle of a killing frost or the roar of a wildfire.

Human teachings that place emotions on a spectrum of bad to good are ridiculous — much like your petty declarations that one day's weather passes muster while another is dreary, nasty, or simply should not be. How pathetic it is to rail against such forces of nature rather than making the most of them and learning to channel the unique beauty and magic they contain.

If you try pulling back from an emotion, it is like pulling back an arrow in a bow. Your attempt will, at best, postpone its expression while all the while increasing its momentum and range.

Instead, locate and identify your rage. Where is it? Why are you angry, and at whom? It is even possible that you are feeling something akin to hate. Do not hold back. Admitting your feelings to yourself—even your revenge fantasies—hurts no one. And without acknowledging that you hold them, you can never let them go, let alone channel them toward creating positive change.

If you have been trained to believe that nice people don't feel rage or rage is toxic and will cause grievous harm to you and others, waste no time in throwing off the yoke of emotional oppression. These teachings are delusional and naïve and are designed to keep you from knowing yourself truly, which in turn will keep you from your power.

For example, when you are mistreated, it is natural to feel rage. And eventually, in order to properly heal and move on, you must admit those feelings and allow them to flow.

Without rage, citizens would never rise up against dictators or take the steps necessary to alleviate social injustice.

Many a legendary career was chosen out of rage at the existing state of affairs.

Even when your rage might be considered disproportionate or inappropriate, it must be felt before you can channel its wisdom and eventually let it go. Sometimes the healthiest thing for a forest is to burn.

Once you are clear on exactly how you feel, simply feel it. Punch your pillow if you need to. Cry, go somewhere where you can yell and scream, dance to music that mirrors your feelings, create art, or talk to a friend or support person you can trust. Then decide what you want to do next. Make a plan, and take care that it's an ethical one with everyone's best interests in mind. (Be advised that minimizing or sugarcoating your feelings will rarely be in everyone's best interests.)

Let your rage lead you to your courageous determination, and act on it.

37. Welcome, Dread Fury

CHANNEL FIERCENESS INTO POWER.

Banish now all curses, hexes, and unwanted spells that have been placed upon you. Draw upon your fierceness and the purifying wrath of the Goddess to unbind your soul and spirit now and for all time.

Your freedom from oppressive inner patterns only awaits your instantaneous and complete refusal to host them for one moment more.

The patterns to which I refer may include self-criticism, disempowering cultural programming, coercive control from an individual or group, codependency, intimidation, gaslighting, abuse, or any other form of physical, mental, or emotional hijacking.

You are not as impressionable as you have been made to believe. You are not as susceptible to idle whims and wishes. You were not born to play a supporting role in the lives or fantasies of others. You do not deserve to have your power siphoned or your freedom limited. You must choose now to *un*-choose any or all of these things, once and for all.

Find the 'dread fury' within you — the sharp-taloned, black-eyed goddess who will suffer no foolishness or fools. Allow yourself to feel her presence, that arrives like an inferno to incinerate all you will no longer accept. Let her wild liberation burn through you like a glorious explosion followed by an all-consuming fire.

Human culture and human relationships can be battlefields. There are those who would channel your power towards their egotistical agendas. Sometimes, you must work to heal such dynamics through thoughtful counseling and inner exploration. Other times, you must change your circumstances by immediately and utterly refusing. You must display your sharp teeth and scream a loud and piercing "NO" that resonates throughout time and space, causing all that you are un-choosing to retreat and dissolve away.

The fierce and furious Goddess is here for you. She reminds you that you have all the power you need to step out of whatever has been binding you, and you have that power now. Use it, and never look back.

38. The Sea-Maid's Music

HEAL THROUGH CREATIVITY.

The longing within you holds great beauty. To reveal that beauty, channel your pain into art.

It is a great error to believe that a life should be filled with only sunlight and cheerful songs in major keys. It is an expectation that can never be met, and for those who wish to live fully, it is an idea that holds no allure.

Of course, if you do nothing but wallow endlessly in sadness, such behavior will quickly become boring both for others and for you. But hiding your melancholy away from yourself and the world will bring grave stagnation to your inner landscape. It will not fail to fester and become toxic.

Art is the alchemy that transforms your painful emotion into something that heals. Heal yourself and others now by creating music, visual art, poetry, a book, an essay, a story, or a play. Or, perhaps you would prefer to prepare a performance of some kind. Whatever you create, put your heartache into it. Do not edit out or conceal your anger, your loneliness, your fear, or your rage. If you have experienced great tragedy in your past, make sure you find a way to include that too.

There may be immense happiness and hope in your artwork also, but Goddess forbid that is all that you share. To characterize this life experience as anything less than the full spectrum of light and darkness is to prolong your own loneliness and the loneliness of others. To restrict yourself to the bright side is to refuse to look at the truth, which means your life has become a lie.

As you well know, everyone you love will one day die. Everything you love will one day pass away. This gives you reason to mourn, but it also reminds you to enjoy what you have while it lasts. What's more, we are here without explanation — sometimes the mystery inspires, and other times it terrifies. Be brave and embrace it all. And put it all into your work.

You may have an artistic medium already that you practice. But if you don't, choose one now and channel your feelings into it. Do not allow commercialism or a desire for commercial validation to color your choices. Do not start with the thought that you are making a product to sell. Rather, focus on communicating something vital and ineffable.

Find the vein of gold within your dark moods and existential *ennui*. Illuminate it, clarify it, and broadcast it. Find what is universal about it, and share it.

This will set in motion great waves of healing, both within and without.

39. Her Pale Fire

REST. RELAX. RECEIVE.

The sun blazes and burns, sending its blinding, expansive light to the earth. The moon does no such thing. It sits passively, soaking in light from the sun, which it then reflects to us in gentle, mystical rays of healing, nourishment, balance, magic, and restorative rest.

Take a lesson from the moon. If you are looking for an answer to a question about what to do, stop thinking. Rest instead. Find mindful presence and abiding calm. Then, when the time is right, your answer will arise unbidden, and you will know what to do, not just in your mind but also in your body and spirit.

If there is something specific you want—a relationship, object, condition, or outcome—stop chasing after it or wearing yourself out with frenzied activity. Much like the moon, who passively absorbs the radiant light she calmly shares with the world, staying still and cultivating quiet receptivity is the dynamic that will effectively allow you to draw that which you desire into your life experience.

When you chase a cat, you will never catch it. When you sit still and relax, the cat will jump on your lap and happily cuddle up. Stop chasing the cat.

Make yourself some tea. Relax. Take a deep breath. Enjoy your cozy environment. Look out the window at the sky. Take a deep breath. Slowly and extravagantly inhabit your body. Perhaps establish even more comfort and even more luxury if you wish. Let go of extraneous tasks and responsibilities. Revel in your own unique beauty. Smile to yourself and enter into stillness, silence, and space. Take time to take care of yourself and savor the sense that you have all the time in the world.

When you stop desperately searching, ruminating, and pursuing, everything you've been looking for will find you.

40. Love All, Trust a Few

REFUSE TO BE CONTROLLING OR CONTROLLED.

If you mistake universal love for unquestioning trust, there will surely be those who will happily take advantage of your confusion of the two.

You can tune into the eternal nature of a soul—one's inherent beauty and worthiness—without agreeing to go along with everything someone asks, assumes, or appears to require.

It does make sense to love everyone unconditionally if you can manage it. At the same time, you need not let everyone into your inner circle of trust.

Some people you will want to keep at a distance. Still others you may want to bar from your life completely.

This is not a perfect science. No two people are alike. Every relationship is a negotiation of power and an exploration of what feels right and safe to you at this particular time. The older you get, the more experience and wisdom you will gain. But as long as you interact with others, you will not be immune from the attentions of those who will seek to dominate, manipulate, and control.

There may also be times when you are the manipulative party: the abuser, the narcissist, or the boundary crosser. If you find yourself dismissing the previous statement outright, stop. Read it again. Ask yourself, "Have I received such feedback lately?" If so, "Did I refuse to entertain the possibility that I could be mistreating someone? Have I reflected upon my actions and asked myself whether or not I was acting with kindness and integrity?"

As the wise bard wrote, "Love all, trust a few, do wrong to none."

Admitting mistakes makes you stronger, not weaker. Desperately clinging to a vision of yourself as right or perfect is like quicksand, pulling you further and further from honest connection and personal evolution.

And even though the same is true for others—

mistakes or weaknesses do not condemn a person or deem them eternally unworthy of love—this does not mean you must give your precious time and attention to anyone and everyone who asks for it.

Protect your energy by following the humble and intuitive voice within. Enforce the boundaries that feel right to you, whether those boundaries will serve to modify a relationship or end it entirely.

Love all. Send your love out universally. But trust no more than a few. And harm no one. Honestly examine your own behavior and even question your own perhaps overly flattering self-image when appropriate. And don't hesitate to amend or permanently terminate any relationship you choose. You do not need to defend or explain your choice. The fact that you have chosen is enough.

41. The Forgeries of Jealousy

STEP OUT OF THE ILLUSION.

Jealousy, envy, or comparison is currently coloring your perspective and showing you an unreal vision of the world and your place in it.

As a social creature, it is natural to compare yourself to others. But sometimes, you become blinded by the false narratives that arise in response to these comparisons. This is what is happening now.

Extricating yourself from this mental trap is actually quite simple, and it can even be instantaneous. Here's how: question the story you are telling. And tell yourself a new one.

For example, you may believe that when someone is thriving according to external and measurable factors, they are thriving exactly as much as they appear to be. They have no problems, and everything is permanently great for them. Believing this story sets you up to feel that you can never measure up. In fact, this is never true. Everyone suffers, and everyone has challenges you cannot see.

Or, you may believe that if someone else has something you want, it makes it less likely that you can *also* have what you want. But someone else having something you want is actually proof that you can have what you want. Change the story, and your experience will change. Smile and say to yourself, "What the Goddess has provided for ____, She now provides for me and more."

Sometimes, your jealousy may fabricate a story that a friend or significant other is being deceitful or loves someone else more than they love you. That's why, before you react, it's important to take the time to discover what is *actually* true rather than what your jealousy attempts to convince you is true.

Regardless of the form the forgery may take, the reality is that you have plenty, the world is beautiful, and there is much to be grateful for. The more you believe this, the truer it gets. So you need not be miserly about love, abundance, belongings, or anything else, for as one wind of fortune recedes, another is already on its way. Worry not and fret no longer about what others are experiencing. Look instead to the endless breezes of blessings continuously blowing your way.

Do not wait. At this very moment, remove your focus from the illusion of lack and open your eyes to the reality of your luck. What you choose to see will multiply.

42. Venus in the Sky

BE MAGNETIC.

You possess a uniquely mesmerizing beauty. Embody it now for your own personal enjoyment and to bless the world with divine light.

Venus is the Goddess of Love and the brightest planet in the sky. In both these roles, she both receives and broadcasts radiance. It is as if she is swimming in an ocean of brilliance — absorbing it, sharing it, and reveling in it. As she both bathes in and blesses the world with divine luminosity, she leverages these polarities of receiving and giving to continually increase her own glorious glow.

Be a devotee of your own magnificence. Cherish the goddess-like beauty within you. Cleanse away anything that limits your shine. Patiently coax your inherent sparkle with relaxation, inspiration, self-adornment, and self-care.

Essentially, you must now find the energy of magnetism, sweetness, and attraction within you. You can then easily use that energy to draw love, romance, attention, abundance, and anything else you desire.

The Goddess of Love does not restrict her charms to the young or conventionally attractive. She blesses and dwells within us all. We can all call on her and utilize her magic. This intrinsic current of romance can inspire us to take exciting chances, make positive changes, and see and experience the mystery and majesty of life and existence.

No matter what your question or current situation, your answer is this: access the quality of divine beauty within. Invoke the Love Goddess, surrender to her, and let her take over. Fall in love with nature, with music, with colors, with textures, and with scents. Slowly savor smooth chocolate or sweet fruit. Sway to a hypnotic beat. Gaze at the sunlight dancing on the sea. Once you are well and truly flowing and shining with the Goddess' beauty, your momentum will effortlessly carry you toward the sweetest and loveliest of lands.

43. Raging Fire of Fever

Channel your passion.

Passion is the fire that illuminates your world.

Ground that passion now. Hold it. Keep it burning steadily by allowing it to flow through the earth, your body, and the present moment.

When fire is suppressed, it eventually burns out. When it is allowed to burn out of control, it devastates. But when fire is contained and consciously channeled toward a positive purpose, it grants life, warmth, and the power to do great things.

Do not extinguish your passion, but do not let

it be a wildfire. Smother it, and you will lose the thread of your joy — in work, spirituality, friendships, and romance. Carelessly let it spread, and you will experience self-destructiveness, addiction, unhealthy relationships, and challenging mental and physical health.

Properly directed, the flame of passion is the ideal fuel for inspiration, connection, success, creation, expansion, and self-growth.

Take time each day to breathe consciously. Sensitize yourself to gravity and the feeling of your body on the earth. Align with all the elements: earth, air, fire, water, and spirit. Notice where more balance might be established and take steps to develop it. Create space in your mind and relax your body. Set clear intentions in every life area.

Sense your natural enthusiasm like an ever-burning pilot light within you. Tend to that flame like the priestesses of Vesta — let it be a fire of devotion at the altar of your heart. Then deliberately send that blinding radiance into all the energetic pathways and conduits that stoke and light up your desires.

You are a force of nature, and you are also an alchemical engineer. Be clear-minded and purposeful in your use of power. Bathe in the brightness of your passion and let it be the spark that steadily kindles your commitment, connection, excellence, and works of fabulous genius.

44. Follow Darkness Like a Dream

MASTER YOUR FEAR. EXPLORE YOUR SHADOW.

The darkness is sacred. The night holds beautiful secrets. There is a unique healing quality to the cool light of the moon.

One cannot fully appreciate the day without the profound renewal of night. Devotion to life is not complete without devotion, also, to death.

Instead of chasing happiness, frivolity, and light, try following darkness like a dream. Revel in the velvety texture of your sadness. Breathe deeply into your foggy loneliness, and discover a certain pleasure in letting your painful feelings flow. The night does not last forever, after all. Its unique delights are but passing through.

Seek and enjoy the aesthetics of the dark. Wear or decorate with dark colors, moody styles, and gothic imagery, or incorporate them into your artistic medium of choice. Play or listen to music that is mysterious or even macabre.

Value not just your dreams but also your nightmares. There is a vast reserve of power hidden in your fear. Turn towards it, not away. A recurring nightmare, much like a persistent worry, is an opportunity to practice mastering and moving beyond your discomfort and dread. Be willing to look fear in the face again and again for as long as it takes. With each jolt of terror you lean into, your fright will diminish, and your courage will steadily prevail.

Similarly, your sensitivity can feel like a burden when you feel the heartbreak of the world. But when you learn to hold that pain and be with it, your spiritual wisdom will deepen, and your psychic and intuitive abilities will increase.

You can't outrun your shadow, and you can't heal everything or eradicate everyone's suffering. But when you gaze with clear eyes into the dark, you will discover a portal to power.

    Relax into darkness. Flow with it. Follow it like a dream.

45. Dive Into the Fire

LET GO. TRANSFORM. RISE ANEW.

It is time for you to transform and be reborn.

The legendary phoenix ages, wastes away, and dies. It appears certain she will never fly again, move, or even take another breath. And then! There is a spark, a flame, and a raging fire. And from that fire, the phoenix rises — glorious, glowing, and made of light.

Kindle the alchemical fire of transformation now, and enter into it. Let the old die forever and burn away to make room for the new.

Clinging desperately to the past will not bring it

back, just as dead firewood will not once again become a sapling in spring. Release old conditions, relationships, habits, belongings, concepts, paradigms, expectations, approaches, and anything else ready to go. Stop trying to resuscitate it. Let it thoroughly die so it can be the kindling for your glorious rebirth.

This could be a comprehensive message, but it could also be about a single and specific quality or condition in your life: your approach to work, for example, or your living situation. Perhaps it's time to move to a new town or begin a brand new career path.

If you have been feeling joyless or depressed, it's time to proactively shake things up. Get honest with yourself about the ideas and paradigms that have shaped your choices and your world. For example, you may have picked up the idea that you have to live close to your family or prepare for a sane and reasonable job that you don't even like. Look deeply and identify anything you can crumple up and throw onto the flames.

Even a single, seemingly simple change—like the shoes you wear or what you have for breakfast—can act as a spark that eventually sets your world on fire. Especially when you question the unexamined assumptions or patterns that have lent themselves to boredom and self-limitation. What if you're not actually the type to wear sensible shoes or eat the same old thing for breakfast every day? What if you're someone else entirely? Who is that person? Get curious and find out.

Be like the phoenix. Let go of certainty, familiarity, and monotony. Be willing to let what is tired and worn out die, even before you are sure what will arise anew.

Dive into the fire. You will transform and then rise, filled with magnificent light.

ABOUT THE AUTHOR

TESS WHITEHURST believes life is magical. She's the author of three other oracle decks besides this one: *The Oracle of Portals*, *Cosmic Dancer Oracle*, and *The Magic of Flowers Oracle*. (She also has another one in the works.)

Tess' books include the bestselling *Magical Housekeeping*, the award-winning *The Magic of Flowers*, and lots of other fan favorites, such as *The Self-Love Superpower, You Are Magical, The Good Energy Book*, and *The Magic of Trees*. Articles she has written have appeared in *Writer's Digest*, *Spirit & Destiny*, and *Llewellyn's Magical Almanac*. She's appeared on morning shows on both Fox and NBC, and her feng shui work was featured on the Bravo TV show *Flipping Out*.

Tess' teachings about magic and spirituality appear extensively online, particularly on her Youtube channel and her online membership portal, Wisdom Circle Online School of Magical Arts.

Tess lives in the Rocky Mountains of Colorado with a handsome man and a handsome cat.

Find lots of free resources, like guided

meditations, spells, rituals, and motivational pep talks at: **TessWhitehurst.com**

ABOUT THE ARTISTS

MÉLANIE DELON
Mélanie is a freelance illustrator who lives in a small town near Alençon (Normandy, France). She creates illustrations for book covers, has worked for many publishing houses around the world, and created concept arts for the video game industry. Mélanie also has a number of works in progress for magazines specializing in 2D.

In 2007, Mélanie published her first artbook, *Elixir 1* — a collection of illustrations with short stories, followed by the second volume in 2010. The worlds Mélanie seeks to create through her illustrations are based on fantasy—her favourite subject—but she always adds a touch of classicism and romanticism, as she finds mixing styles brings more realism to the painting.

After studying History of Art and Archeology at the Sorbonne, Mélanie went to a 3D school where she discovered digital illustration. She started to work as a freelance illustrator in 2005, by trading her pens and paper for Photoshop and a Wacom graphic tablet.

In 2012, Mélanie decided to try something new by creating her own publishing house/shop EXUVIA. In 2014 she released her third artbook, *Opale 1*, under this label. The second volume will be released in 2023.

Since 2017, Mélanie has taught digital painting at CGMA.

Artwork by Mélanie Delon appears on cards 2, 3, 4, 6, 8, 9, 10, 11, 12, 13, 14, 15, 16, 17, 18, 19, 20, 21, 22, 23, 24, 25, 27, 28, 29, 30, 31, 32, 33, 34, 36, 37, 38, 39, 40, 41, 42, 43, and 45.

Cecilia G.F.

Cecilia has a degree in art history from the University of Malaga, and although she tried to look for a job in another field for a while, she never stopped drawing. A self-taught illustrator, Cecilia uses her knowledge of symbology and art theory in her illustrations to enrich them with meaning. Her inspiration comes from different sources, such as music, books, video games, and mythology, which can be seen in her work.

Cecilia has collaborated with publishers such as Alethé, Supersonic, Nocturna, Kakao Books, and Munyx, among others, and has worked with international clients worldwide.

Some of her best-known works are *CloroFilia* by Cristina Jurado (for which she won the Ignotus Award in 2018), *La Compañía Amable* by Rocío Vega, *Sistemas Críticos* by Martha Wells, or *El clan sin nombre* by África Vázquez Beltrán.

Social networks:
ThanatosofNicte on Twitter, Instagram and Twitch.
Ceciliagf on ArtStation.

Artwork by Cecilia G.F. appears on cards 1, 5, 7, 26, and 35.

Also available from Blue Angel Publishing®

The Oracle of Portals
Traversing Gateways of Power and Possibility

Tess Whitehurst
Artwork by Laila Savolainen

Come beyond the bounds of time and place to discover the profound and transformative power of the in-between. You are forever on the threshold of becoming, and every turn, choice, action, and word is a path maker. Now, you can consciously navigate the liminal to open the gateways to your brighter future.

Journey through and explore the portals of this beautifully illustrated 44-card set, and let your pathway unfold as a glorious expression of your magical self. Be bold, be true — your tomorrow awaits!

ISBN: 978-1-922573-43-8
44 cards and 148-page guidebook set

Also available from Blue Angel Publishing®

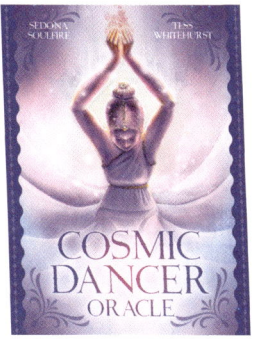

Cosmic Dancer Oracle

Sedona Soulfire &
Tess Whitehurst
Artwork by Elinore Eaton

Engage with the dance of life, animate your soul, and partner with the undulating cadence of the world around you. Activate the cards to bring mindfulness and loving awareness to your entire body, and ask for insight into situations, challenges, relationships, or for general guidance. Each card message includes a simple exercise to help you harmonize with the healing, grace and beauty of the cosmic dance.

ISBN: 978-1-925538-88-5
44 cards and 148-page guidebook set

Also available from Blue Angel Publishing®

Practical Magic
An Oracle for Everyday Enchantment

Serene Conneeley
Artwork by Selina Fenech

Energise the purpose, knowledge, and potential within you to empower your heart and transform your tomorrows. This inspired collaboration is a rich compendium of fascination, insight, ritual, symbolism, and divination that you can action in your daily life for surprising and satisfying results.

Journey into initiation and possibility, welcome adventure and reward, set nurturing boundaries, and shape your reality with the support of deities, herbs, crystals, colour, the elements, and intention. Believe in your innate powers of creation and innovation, and charge your world with wonder — now and always.

ISBN: 978-1-922573-70-4
36 cards and 304-page guidebook set + card stand

Also available from Blue Angel Publishing®

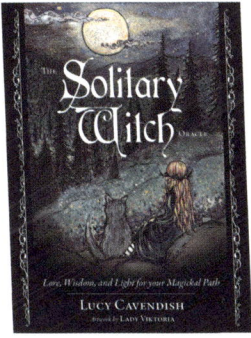

The Solitary Witch Oracle
Lore, Wisdom, and Light for Your Magickal Path

Lucy Cavendish
Artwork by Lady Viktoria

Wherever there are humans, there are solitary witches — independent emissaries of magick who love others but adore the companionship of the free and the wild even more.

This enchanting oracle is an illuminating tapestry of insight, comfort, healing, and practical guidance for awakening your charms and senses. Together, the spark of Lucy Cavendish's prose and Lady Viktoria's alluring hand-painted imagery evoke profound rememberings to draw back the veil and celebrate your magickal soul.

Your new journey begins ...

ISBN: 978-1-922573-50-6
45 cards and 180-page guidebook set

For more information on this
or any Blue Angel Publishing® release,
please visit our website at:

www.blueangelonline.com